How Sweet the Sound

AFRICAN-AMERICAN SONGS FOR CHILDREN

Selected by Wade and Cheryl Hudson
Illustrated by Floyd Cooper

SCHOLASTIC INC.
New York Toronto London Auckland Sydney

—For our ancestors, who paved the way—
W.H. and C.H.

—For my grandpa, C.D. Williams—
F.C.

The text is set in Cheltenham. The display type is Garamond Bold Italic.

Book design by Cheryl Willis Hudson.
Music engraving by Randa Kirshbuam.

ISBN 0-590-48034-0

12 11 10 9 8 7

0 1 2/0

Printed in the U.S.A.

14

Contents

Introduction

When we were children growing up in the South, Black music was all around us. Our parents sang as they did chores around the house. Bluesmen sat on porches, crooning and playing their guitars. Teenagers stood on street corners and harmonized to the latest hit tunes. Choirs and gospel groups lifted their voices in churches. Students performed in talent shows in schools. Yes, there was music everywhere.

Music has always been an integral part of African-American life because it serves many purposes. It records history. It unites people, protests wrongs, and helps one endure tough times. It raises the spirit and cleanses the soul. It celebrates life.

Could African Americans have endured slavery without the spirituals and chants they used to empower their spirits? Would the Civil Rights movement have been as effective without the freedom songs that helped to motivate and inspire supporters? It is difficult to imagine African-American life without music.

African-American traditions in music owe much to the African influence. Africans who were captured and taken to America to serve as slaves brought with them their memories of a rich African culture. That culture included the importance of music and the function music served as a communal activity. This legacy has been passed down to subsequent generations.

How Sweet the Sound gives readers a glimpse at the history of Blacks in America through their music. Key periods are spotlighted by a variety of songs. There are songs from Africa, spirituals, work songs, gospels, jazz, blues songs, play songs, chants, soul, and popular music of our own time.

Like its companion, *Pass It On: African-American Poetry for Children,* this volume is brought to life by award-winning illustrator Floyd Cooper. His richly colored paintings beautifully depict each era in African-American history and capture the love, sorrows, determination, and triumphs of Black America.

How Sweet the Sound has been truly a labor of love. Our work on this book has taught us more about our own experience. It is a book for the entire family to read, to sing along with, to learn from, and enjoy. And is there a more enjoyable way to learn than through music?

Wade Hudson
Cheryl Hudson
1995

Kum Ba Ya

TRADITIONAL

Kum ba ya. Ya.
Kum ba ya. Ya.
Kum ba ya. Ya.
Kum ba ya. Ya.
Kum ba ya. Ya.
Kum ba ya. Ya.
Ah, ah. Kum ba ya.

Come by here, my Lord, come by here.
Come by here, my Lord, come by here.
Come by here, my Lord, come by here.
Oh Lord, come by here.

Over My Head

SPIRITUAL

Over my head, I hear music in the air.
Over my head, I hear music in the air.
Over my head, I hear music in the air.
There must be a God somewhere.

Over my head, I hear singing in the air.
Over my head, I hear singing in the air.
Over my head, I hear singing in the air.
There must be a God somewhere.

Over my head, I see trouble in the air.
Over my head, I see trouble in the air.
Over my head, I see trouble in the air.
There must be a God somewhere.

Over my head, I see glory in the air.
Over my head, I see glory in the air.
Over my head, I see glory in the air.
There must be a God somewhere.

Go Down, Moses

SPIRITUAL

When Israel was in Egypt's land,
Let my people go.
Oppressed so hard they could not stand,
Let my people go.

Chorus
Go down, Moses.
Way down in Egypt's land.
Tell old Pharaoh
Let my people go.

"Thus spoke the Lord," bold Moses said,
"Let my people go!
If not, I'll smite your firstborn dead.
Let my people go!"

"No more shall they in bondage toil,
Let my people go!
Let them come out with Egypt's spoil.
Let my people go!"

Follow the Drinkin' Gourd

TRADITIONAL

Follow the drinkin' gourd!
Follow the drinkin' gourd.
For the Ole Man is a-waitin' for to carry you to freedom
If you follow the drinkin' gourd.

When the sun comes back and the first quail calls,
Follow the drinkin' gourd,
For the Ole Man is a-waitin' for to carry you to freedom
If you follow the drinkin' gourd.

Oh, the river bank makes a mighty good road.
Dead trees will mark the way.
The left foot, peg foot, travelin' on.
Follow the drinkin' gourd.

Where the river ends in between two hills
Follow the drinkin' gourd.
There the Ole Man is a-waitin' for to carry you to freedom
If you follow the drinkin' gourd.

Take This Hammer

TRADITIONAL

Take this hammer, (huh!)
Carry it to the captain, (huh!)
Take this hammer, (huh!)
Carry it to the captain, (huh!)
Take this hammer, (huh!)
Carry it to the captain, (huh!)
Tell him I'm gone, (huh!)
Tell him I'm gone. (huh!)

If he asks you, (huh!)
Was I running, (huh!)
If he asks you, (huh!)
Was I running, (huh!)
If he asks you, (huh!)
Was I running, (huh!)
Tell him I was flying, (huh!)
Tell him I was flying. (huh!)

If he asks you, (huh!)
Was I laughing, (huh!)
If he asks you, (huh!)
Was I laughing, (huh!)
If he asks you, (huh!)
Was I laughing, (huh!)
Tell him I was crying, (huh!)
Tell him I was crying. (huh!)

Repeat first verse.

Bring Me Li'l' Water, Silvy

HUDDIE LEDBETTER

Bring me little water, Silvy
Bring me little water now.
Bring me little water, Silvy
Every little once in a while.

Can't you hear me callin' you?
Can't you hear me now?
I need a little bit of water
Every little once in a while.

Silvy come a-runnin'
Bucket in her hand.
I will bring you water
Fast as I can.

Sweet Oranges

STREET CRY

Sweet oranges,
Sweeter than the honey
in the comb.
Sweet oranges!

Blueberries

STREET CRY

Blueberries, fresh and fine.
I got juicy blueberries, lady,
So fresh and fine.
Three baskets for a dime, lady.
Blueberries!
Fresh blueberries!

That's How the Cake Walk's Done

ORIGINAL WORDS AND MUSIC BY J. LEUBRIE HILL
NEW WORDS ADAPTED BY WADE HUDSON

The Cake Walking craze,
It's a fad now-a-days
With black folks and white folks, too.
And I really declare
It's done everywhere
Though it may be something new to you.
'Twas introduced years ago way down South you know
By black folks from Tennessee.
So just to show you
I'm going to do
A Cake Walk of a high degree.

Bow to the right,
Bow to the left,
Then you proudly take your place.
Be sure to have a smile on your face.
Step high with lots of style and grace.
With a salty prance
Do a ragtime dance.
Step way back, get ready for fun.
With a bow look wise.
Flutter your eyes.
For that's the way the Cake Walk's done.

The Boll Weevil

HUDDIE LEDBETTER

Talk about the latest, the latest of this song,
These devilish boll weevils, they gonna rob you of a home;
They lookin' for a home, they lookin' for a home.
I'll have a home, I'll have a home.

The first time I saw him, he was settin' on a square,
The next time I saw him, he had his whole family there;
He was lookin' for a home, he was lookin' for a home.

The farmer and his old lady went out across the field,
The farmer said to his old lady, "I found a lot of meat and meal,
I'll have a home, I'll have a home."

The old lady said to the old man, "I'm tryin' my level best
To keep these devilish boll weevils out of my brand-new cotton dress;
It's full of holes, it's full of holes."

The farmer said to the old lady, "What do you think of that?
I got one of them boll weevils out of my brand-new Stetson hat.
It's full of holes, it's full of holes."

The farmer took the boll weevil, put him in the sand,
Boll weevil said to the farmer, "You treat me just like a man—
I'll have a home, I'll have a home."

The farmer took the boll weevil, put him on the ice,
Boll weevil said to the farmer, "You're treatin' me mighty nice—
I'll have a home, I'll have a home."

Farmer told the merchant, "I didn't make but one bale,
Before I let you have that one, I'll suffer an' die in jail;
I'll have a home, I'll have a home."

Lift Ev'ry Voice and Sing

WORDS BY JAMES WELDON JOHNSON
MUSIC BY J. ROSAMOND JOHNSON

Lift ev'ry voice and sing,
Till earth and heaven ring.
Ring with the harmonies of Liberty;
Let our rejoicing rise,
High as the list'ning skies,
Let it resound loud as the rolling sea.
Sing a song full of the faith that the dark past has taught us,
Sing a song full of the hope that the present has brought us;
Facing the rising sun of our new day begun,
Let us march on till victory is won.

Stony the road we trod,
Bitter the chast'ning rod,
Felt in the days when hope unborn had died;
Yet with a steady beat,
Have not our weary feet,
Come to the place for which our fathers sighed?
We have come over a way that with tears has been watered,
We have come, treading our path thro' the blood of the slaughtered,
Out from the gloomy past, till now we stand at last
Where the white gleam of our bright star is cast.

God of our weary years,
God of our silent tears,
Thou who has brought us thus far on the way;
Thou who hast by Thy might,
Led us into the light,
Keep us forever in the path, we pray.
Lest our feet stray from the places, our God, where we met Thee,
Lest our hearts, drunk with the wine of the world, we forget Thee;
Shadowed beneath Thy hand, may we forever stand,
True to our God, true to our native land.

Swing Low, Sweet Chariot

SPIRITUAL

Swing low, sweet chariot,
Comin' for to carry me home.
Swing low, sweet chariot,
Comin' for to carry me home.

I looked over Jordan and what did I see,
Comin' for to carry me home?
A band of angels comin' after me,
Comin' for to carry me home.

Swing low, sweet chariot,
Comin' for to carry me home.
Swing low, sweet chariot,
Comin' for to carry me home.

If you get there before I do,
Comin' for to carry me home,
Tell all my friends I'm coming too,
Comin' for to carry me home.

Sometimes I'm up, sometimes I'm down,
Comin' for to carry me home.
But still my soul is heaven bound,
Comin' for to carry me home.

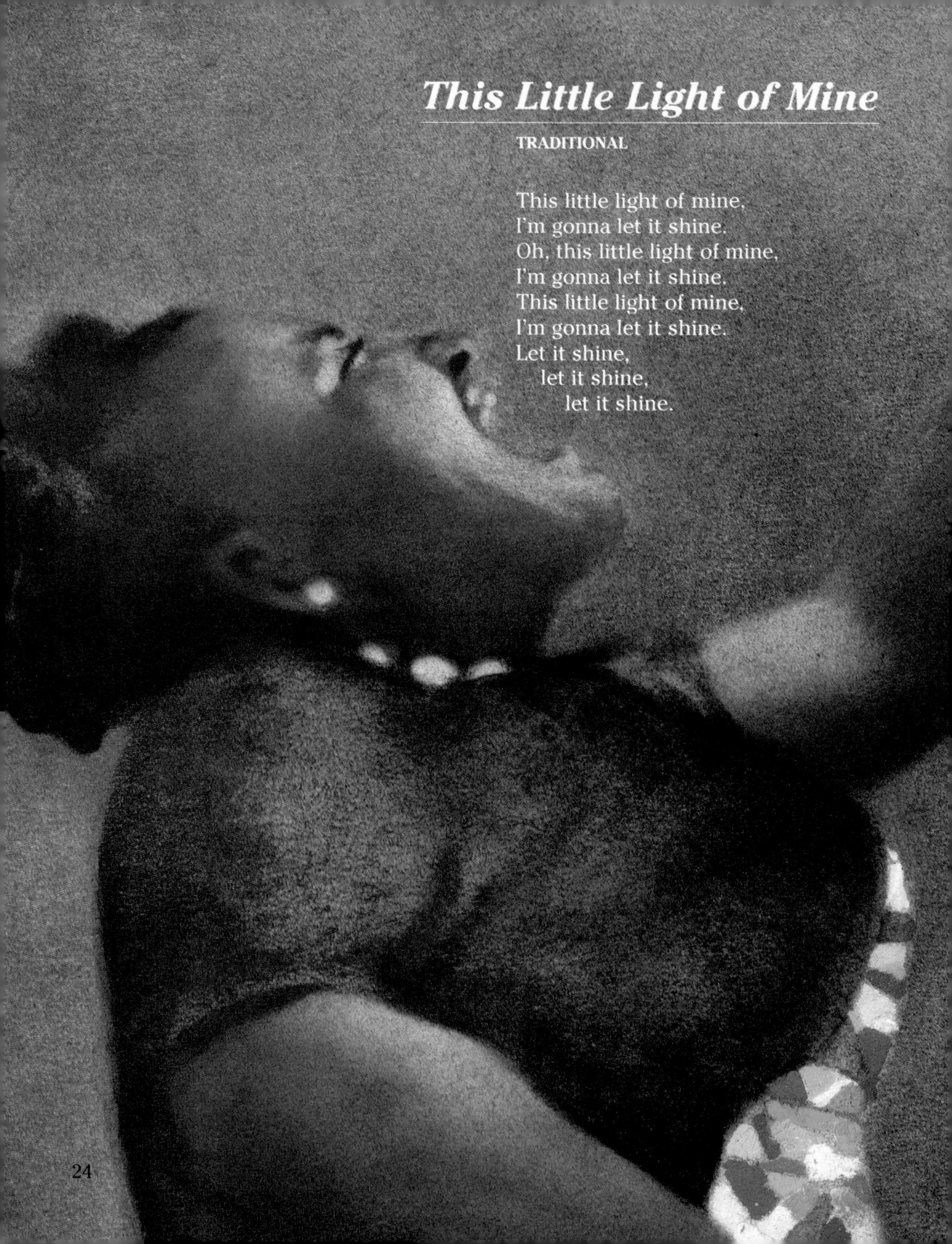

This Little Light of Mine

TRADITIONAL

This little light of mine,
I'm gonna let it shine.
Oh, this little light of mine,
I'm gonna let it shine.
This little light of mine,
I'm gonna let it shine.
Let it shine,
let it shine,
let it shine.

Take My Hand, Precious Lord

THOMAS A. DORSEY

Precious Lord, take my hand.
Lead me on, let me stand.
I am tired, I am weak, I am worn.
Thru the storm, thru the night,
Lead me on to the light.
Take my hand, precious Lord,
Lead me on.

When my way grows drear,
Precious Lord linger near.
When life is almost gone,
Hear my cry, hear my call,
Hold my hand lest I fall,
Take my hand, precious Lord,
Lead me on.

Take the "A" Train

BILLY STRAYHORN

If you want to go to Harlem
'Way up to Sugar Hill
Where those dancing feet
You read of
Are never, never still,
Then you must take the "A" Train
To go to Sugar Hill
'Way up in Harlem.

If you miss the "A" Train
You'll find you've missed
The quickest way to Harlem.

Hurry, get on.
Now it's comin'.
Listen to those rails a-thrumming.

All 'board! Get on the "A" Train.
Soon you will be
On Sugar Hill in Harlem.

Miss Mary Mack

TRADITIONAL/HAND-CLAPPING SONG

Miss Mary Mack, Mack, Mack,
All dressed in black, black, black,
With silver buttons, buttons, buttons,
All down her back, back, back.

She asked her mother, mother, mother,
For fifteen cents, cents, cents,
To see the elephant, elephant, elephant,
Jump over the fence, fence, fence.

He jumped so high, high, high,
That he reached the sky, sky, sky,
And he didn't come back, back, back,
Till the Fourth of July, 'ly, 'ly.

Hambone

TRADITIONAL/CHANT

Hambone, Hambone where you been?
'Round the world and back again!

Hambone, Hambone where's your wife?
In the kitchen cooking rice.

Hambone, Hambone have you heard?
Papa's gonna buy me a mockingbird.

If that mockingbird don't sing,
Papa's gonna buy me a diamond ring.

If that diamond ring don't shine,
Papa's gonna buy me a fishing line.

Hambone, Hambone where you been?
'Round the world and I'm going again!

Dog, Dog

JAMES BEVEL AND BERNARD LAFAYETTE

Dog dog d-dog a dig-a-dog dog!
Dog dog d-dog a dig-a-dog dog!
Dog dog d-dog a dig-a-dog dog!
Dog dog d-dog a dig-a-dog dog!

If my dog love your dog and your dog love my dog
And my dog love your dog and your dog love my dog
Then why can't we sit under the apple tree?

We Shall Not Be Moved

TRADITIONAL/FREEDOM SONG

We shall not, we shall not be moved.
We shall not, we shall not be moved.
Just like a tree, planted by the water,
We shall not be moved.

We are fighting for our freedom.
We shall not be moved.
We are fighting for our freedom.
We shall not be moved.
Just like a tree, planted by the water,
We shall not be moved.

We are black and white together.
We shall not be moved.
We are black and white together.
We shall not be moved.
Just like a tree, planted by the water,
We shall not be moved.

We will stand and fight together.
We shall not be moved.
We will stand and fight together.
We shall not be moved.
Just like a tree, planted by the water,
We shall not be moved.

Freedom's Comin'

TRADITIONAL/FREEDOM SONG

Chorus

Freedom, Freedom!
Freedom's comin' and it won't be long.
Freedom, Freedom!
Freedom's comin' and it won't be long.
Freedom, Freedom!

We took a trip on a Greyhound bus,
Freedom's comin' and it won't be long.
To fight segregation, this we must.
Freedom's comin' and it won't be long.

We took a trip down Alabama way,
Freedom's comin' and it won't be long.
We met a lot of violence on Mother's Day.
Freedom's comin' and it won't be long.

Violence in 'bama didn't stop our cause.
Freedom's comin' and it won't be long.
Federal marshals come enforce the laws.
Freedom's comin' and it won't be long.

Well, on to Mississippi with speed we go,
Freedom's comin' and it won't be long.
Blue-shirted policemen meet us at the door.
Freedom's comin' and it won't be long.

Well, you can hinder me here and hinder me there,
Freedom's comin' and it won't be long.
But I go right down on my knees in prayer.
Freedom's comin' and it won't be long.

Say It Loud, I'm Black and I'm Proud

JAMES BROWN

Chorus

Say it loud:
"I'm Black and I'm Proud!"
Say it loud:
"I'm Black and I'm Proud!"
Say it loud:
"I'm Black and I'm Proud!"

Some people say we got a lot of malice.
Some say we got a lot of nerve.
But I say we won't quit moving
Until we get what we deserve.

We've been 'buked and we've been scorned.
We've been treated bad, talked about,
As sure as you're born.

But just as sure as it takes two eyes to make a pair,
Brother, we can't quit until we get our share.

I've worked on jobs, with my feet and my hands.
All that work I did was for the other man.
Now we demand a chance to do things for ourselves.
We're tired of beating our heads against the wall
and working for someone else.

Now we demand a chance to do things for ourselves.
We're tired of beating our heads against the wall
and working for someone else.
We're people, we're like the birds and the bees.
We'd rather die on our feet, than live on our knees.

Happy Birthday

STEVIE WONDER

You know it doesn't make much sense.
There oughta be a law against anyone who takes offense
At a day in your celebration.
'Cause we should know in our minds
That there oughta be a time
That we can set aside to show just how much we love you.
And I'm sure you would agree.
What could fit more perfectly
Than to have a world party
On the day you came to be.

Chorus

Happy birthday to ya,
Happy birthday to ya,
Happy birthday.

Happy birthday to ya,
Happy birthday to ya,
Happy birthday.

Get on Board, Little Children

SPIRITUAL

The Gospel train's a-comin',
I hear it just at hand,
I hear the car wheels moving,
And rumbling thro' the land.

Chorus

Get on board, little children,
Get on board, little children,
Get on board, little children,
For there's room for many a more.

I hear the bell and whistle,
A-coming 'round the curve;
She's playing all her steam and pow'r
And straining every nerve.

No signal for another train
To follow on the line;
O sinner, you're forever lost,
If once you're left behind.

The fare is cheap and all can go,
The rich and poor are there;
No second-class on board the train,
No difference in the fare.

About the Songs and Composers

How Sweet the Sound is not a musical song book. It is a picture book that illustrates songs. Therefore, we have provided additional information below to help the reader better understand the African-American music presented.

There are key elements that characterize almost all African-American music. Among them are call and response, the "blue note," the pentatonic scale, 4/4 meter, compelling rhythms, performance style, and the oral tradition. These elements are used in various combinations within the African-American music forms such as jazz, blues, gospel, and soul.

The versions of songs selected for *How Sweet the Sound* may be unfamiliar to some readers. That is because improvisation is also a key component in African-American music. Words to songs are sometimes changed from setting to setting, and so are musical notes.

The notation provided below is in the form of simple melodic lines, intended for the human voice, along with the chords for guitar or piano. The descriptive copy provides a backdrop for each song. For more information about African-American music, a recommended reading and listening list is included on page 46.

Kum Ba Ya **(TRADITIONAL)**
Though its specific origins are not known, this song is thought to have been brought to the United States from West Africa by slaves. Another theory is that the African-American song "Come By Here" was brought to West Africa by African-American missionaries or by freed slaves who migrated to Liberia in the 1800s. When sung by some African-American congregations, the words "Come by here," sound like "Kum ba ya."

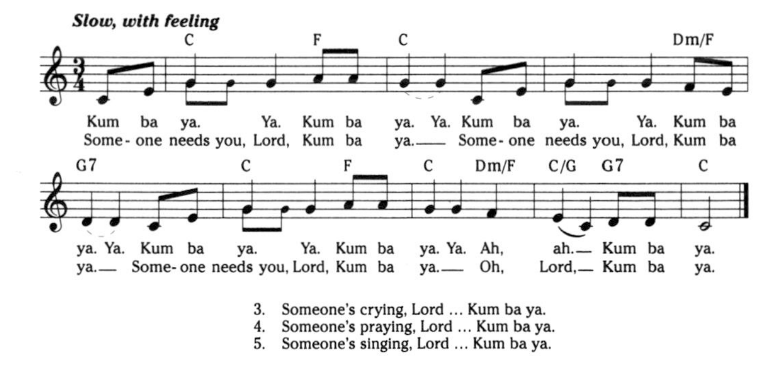

Over My Head **(SPIRITUAL)**
In order to face the horrible conditions of slavery, many African Americans found strength through their belief in God. "Over My Head" is a traditional *spiritual* that illustrates their faith in God, and their hopes that He would one day bring about a change in their lives. Decades after slavery, the lyrics of this song would change to reflect the desire for equality and freedom from segregation during the Civil Rights movement of the 1960s.

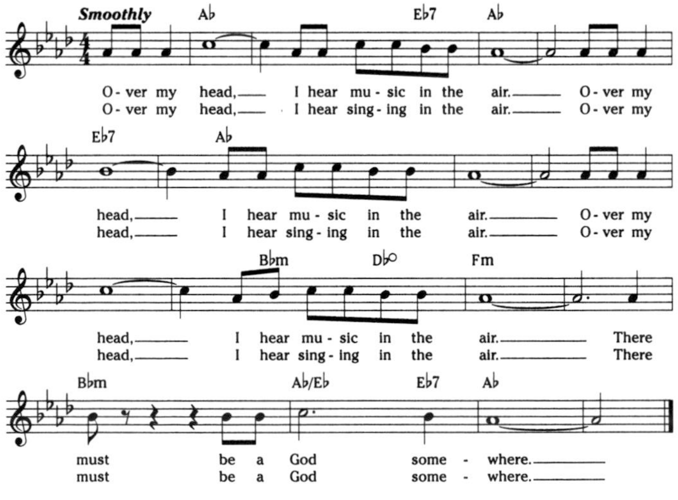

3. Over my head, I see trouble in the air ...
4. Over my head, I see glory in the air ...

Go Down, Moses **(SPIRITUAL)**

Enslaved African Americans wrote many songs about freedom, often choosing biblical heroes to represent their own struggle against slavery. The story of Moses leading the Hebrews out of bondage in Egypt carried its own meaning for slaves who hoped to escape to freedom in the North. The "Moses" of African-American slaves was a woman named Harriet Tubman, whose courageous efforts led many of her people to freedom along the Underground Railroad.

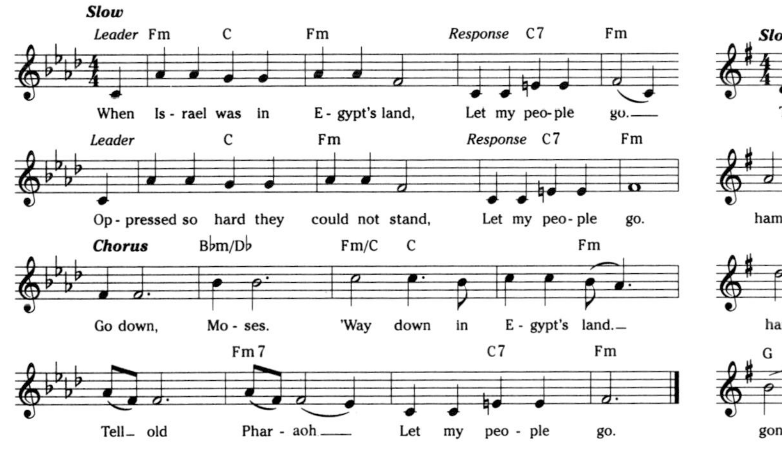

Take This Hammer **(TRADITIONAL/WORK SONG)**

Work songs were sung by African Americans during their long days of back-breaking labor, a tradition brought to America by Africans who were forced into slavery. Whether sung in the cotton fields, while laying railroad tracks, building roads, or digging canals, the rhythm of the songs and the powerful lyrics combined to make the work more bearable. "Take This Hammer" was made popular by African-American folksinger and songwriter, Huddie Ledbetter, also known as Leadbelly (1888 – 1949).

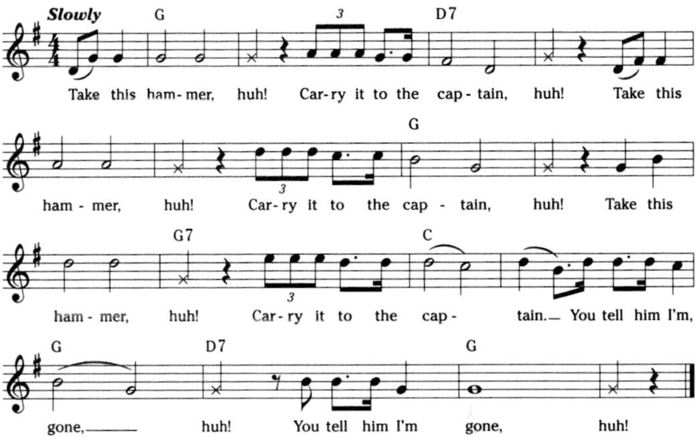

Follow the Drinkin' Gourd **(TRADITIONAL)**

In addition to drawing strength from their songs of freedom, African-American slaves also used these songs to help them escape to the North. Because discovery of an escape plan meant severe punishment or death, the slaves had to disguise their communication in song. The lyrics of "Follow the Drinkin' Gourd" were probably used as directions that guided slaves toward freedom. To "follow the drinkin' gourd" actually meant to follow the constellation of stars known as the Big Dipper.

Bring Me Li'l' Water, Silvy **(WORK SONG)**

Work songs often commented on, and even protested against, horrible work conditions. Written by Leadbelly, "Bring Me Li'l' Water, Silvy" recalls the long, hot summer days when African Americans worked in the fields till near exhaustion, singing of such basic human needs as a drink of water.

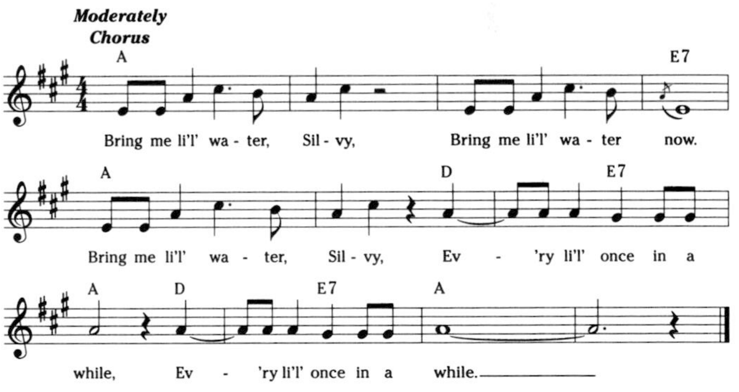

Sweet Oranges **(STREET CRY)**

Whether in celebration or sorrow, music has always played a prominent role in all areas of African-American communities. *Street cries* were functional tunes sung by merchants to help sell their produce. Those songs that seemed to sell the most merchandise became traditional street cries. These two cries were collected and adapted by J. Rosamond Johnson (1873–1954), a leading composer of the early twentieth century.

That's How the Cake Walk's Done **(RAGTIME)**

Begun on plantations during slavery, the Cake Walk became very popular during the late 1800s when the syncopated off-beat rhythm of *ragtime* was introduced. The Cake Walk was actually a dance competition, so named because the first place winner usually received a cake as a prize. "That's How the Cake Walk's Done" was written by J. Leubrie Hill (1889–1916) and was featured in the Black musical *In Dahomey* (London, 1903), whose chief composer was Will Marion Cook (1869–1944).

Blueberries **(STREET CRY)**

Lift Ev'ry Voice and Sing **(HYMN)**

"Lift Ev'ry Voice and Sing" was first sung in honor of Abraham Lincoln's birthday on February 12, 1900. Written by J. Rosamond Johnson and his brother, poet and writer James Weldon Johnson (1871–1938), the song is known today as the Black National Anthem. Following their history through song, "Lift Ev'ry Voice and Sing" is a moving tribute to the hopes, courage, and triumphs of the African-American people.

The Boll Weevil **(BLUES/FOLK SONG)**
Following the oral storytelling tradition of African Americans, "The Boll Weevil" relates the story of the dreaded bug that fed on the cotton plant and made life very difficult for farmers. "The Boll Weevil," written by Leadbelly, is one of the most popular songs in the blues style, which first emerged in the late 1800s. Musician W. C. Handy (1873–1958), known as the "Father of the Blues," is credited with bringing this style of music to a wider audience.

Swing Low, Sweet Chariot **(SPIRITUAL)**
Many spirituals gave hope to African-American slaves because they focused on heaven, where slavery did not exist. Strong faith in God and a belief that a better life awaited them gave many slaves the courage to continue their struggle. For some, the "home" in "Swing Low, Sweet Chariot" could only be heaven, as they had no hope for change in this world. But others dreamed of their own heaven on earth, when slavery would one day be abolished.

This Little Light of Mine **(TRADITIONAL/GOSPEL)**
Gospel music, which emerged in the early 1900s, combines elements from spirituals, hymns, and the blues. Gospel songs and spirituals play an important role in African-American religious services. Songs such as "This Little Light of Mine" contain inspirational lyrics that praise God and enhance the worship experience. "This Little Light of Mine" was a favorite song of civil rights activist Fannie Lou Hamer (1917–1977), who used the song to inspire black sharecroppers to register to vote in the 1960s.

Take My Hand, Precious Lord **(GOSPEL)**
Many gospel songs draw on traditional spirituals, which have a strong African influence. Normally, they are sung by a "leader" who is followed by a congregation or chorus. Composer/arranger/singer Thomas A. Dorsey (1899–1993), known as the "Father of Black Gospel Music," helped to popularize this musical style by touring the country with his choir. "Take My Hand, Precious Lord," written in 1932, is one of the most popular of his nearly one thousand songs.

Miss Mary Mack **(TRADITIONAL/HAND-CLAPPING SONG)**
Some of the *hand-clapping songs* heard on playgrounds today can be traced back to the plantations of the South during slavery. Enslaved African-American children sang these songs, which use rhythmic clapping, to entertain themselves when they were not working in the fields. "Miss Mary Mack" is one of the most popular of these play songs.

Hambone **(TRADITIONAL/CHANT)**
Rhythm has always been basic to African music, but slaves in America were not allowed to have rhythm instruments such as drums. Instead, they used their hands, feet, sticks, or any object they could find to beat out the rhythm of their songs. Clapping *chants* such as "Hambone" reflect the resourcefulness of the African-American slaves.

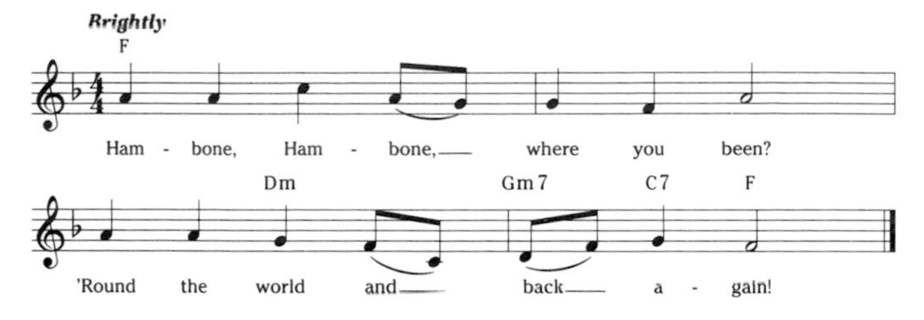

Take the "A" Train **(JAZZ)**
Beginning in New Orleans, Louisiana, in the early 1900s, *jazz* is sometimes called the only truly indigenous American art form. Jazz was born when the instrumental style of ragtime combined with the vocal melodies of the blues. This fresh, new musical style was made popular by such great African-American musicians as Louis Armstrong, Duke Ellington, Fletcher Henderson, King Oliver, and Fats Waller. "Take the 'A' Train," written by Billy Strayhorn (1915–1967), was popularized by his close collaborator, Duke Ellington, and Duke's famous jazz orchestra.

We Shall Not Be Moved **(TRADITIONAL/FREEDOM SONG)**
Whether as an expression of outrage over existing conditions, or as a means of bringing protesters together, freedom songs played an important role in the Civil Rights movement of the 1960s. Often the lyrics of a traditional song were changed to capture the feelings of the protesters. The lyrics of "We Shall Not Be Moved," originally a gospel tune, were rewritten by members of the Student Nonviolent Coordinating Committee (SNCC), an important civil rights organization.

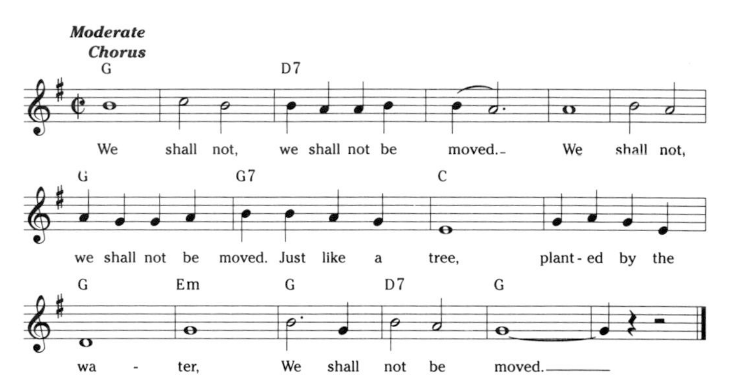

Dog, Dog **(FREEDOM SONG)**
Some freedom songs had simple lyrics, but they did not fail to make powerful statements about the treatment of African-American people. "Dog, Dog," written by civil rights activists James Bevel and Bernard LaFayette, is a good example. The song was inspired by the childhood experience of Bevel, who was not allowed to play with his neighbor's children because they were white. Bevel saw that his neighbor's dog and his own dog were able to play together, and wrote this song to ask the simple question, "Why?"

Freedom's Comin' **(FREEDOM SONG)**
On the importance of songs to the Civil Rights movement, Dr. Martin Luther King, Jr. (1929–1968) said, "The Freedom songs are playing a strong and vital role in our struggle. They give the people new courage and a sense of unity. I think they keep alive a faith, a radiant hope in the future, particularly in our most trying hour." The lyrics to "Freedom's Comin'" were written by "Freedom Riders" who had escaped the fire-bombing of an Alabama Greyhound bus in 1961.

Freedom's Comin'

Say It Loud, I'm Black and I'm Proud **(SOUL)**

During the 1950s and 1960s, a new type of music combining gospel and blues emerged. It was called *soul* and singer/songwriter James Brown, called the "Godfather of Soul," helped to make this style of music popular, earning nearly 50 gold records during his career. The Civil Rights movement and Black nationalism had stirred feelings of Black pride in African-American people. James Brown (1928–) captured that feeling in his 1968 recording of "Say It Loud, I'm Black and I'm Proud." The song became a theme for many African Americans.

Happy Birthday **(SOUL/POPULAR MUSIC)**

As the freedom songs of the 1960s showed, music can successfully help to promote a cause. This fact was again proven in the 1980s, when many Americans fought for a national holiday to honor noted civil rights leader Dr. Martin Luther King, Jr. Singer and songwriter Stevie Wonder (1950–) was a vocal supporter of this cause, bringing it to the nation's attention by recording "Happy Birthday." Though it faced opposition, a national holiday in honor of Dr. King's birthday was declared in 1986.

Happy Birthday

Get On Board, Little Children **(SPIRITUAL)**

Because many spirituals function as more than just religious songs, they have been used by different people for different purposes. "Get On Board, Little Children" has become a traditional song in folk music and is familiar to school children around the world. It was probably written as a religious song that had political significance. The train could be a gospel train. It could be a train of freedom from slavery. But it is a train that anyone can ride.

Recommended Reading and Listening

Barnwell, Ysaye M. and George Brandon. *Singing in the African American Tradition*. Woodstock, NY: Homespun Tapes, 1989.

Bryan, Ashley. *All Night, All Day: A Child's First Book of African-American Spirituals.* New York: Atheneum, 1991.

Mattox, Cheryl Warren. *Let's Get the Rhythm of the Band, A Child's Introduction to Music from African-American Culture.* Nashville: JGT, 1994.

Mattox, Cheryl Warren. *Shake It to the One That You Love the Best: Play Songs and Lullabies from Black Musical Traditions.* El Sobrante, CA: Warren-Mattox Productions, 1989.

Silverman, Jerry. *Songs of Protest and Civil Rights*. New York and Philadelphia: Chelsea House Publishers, 1992.

Songs of Zion, Supplemental Worship Resources, #12. Nashville, TN: Abingdon Press, 1981.

Southern, Eileen, ed. *Readings in Black American Music.* New York: W. W. Norton, 1971.

Sweet Honey in the Rock. *All For Freedom* (cassette). Redway, CA: Music for Little People, 1989.

Index

The first line of each song appears in italicized print.

Acknowledgments

Every effort has been made to trace the ownership of all copyrighted material and to secure permission to reprint these selections. In the event of any question arising as to the use of any material, the editor and the publisher, while expressing regret for any inadvertent error, will be happy to make the necessary correction in future printings.

We thank the following for permission to reprint the copyrighted materials listed below:

pages 13, 41 "Bring Me Li'l' Water, Silvy," Words and Music by Huddie Ledbetter, collected & adapted by John A. Lomax and Alan Lomax, TRO copyright © 1936 (Renewed) Folkways Music Publishers, Inc., New York, NY. Used by permission.

pages 17, 42 "That's How the Cake Walk's Done," words and music by J. Leubrie Hill, was originally published in the score for the musical, *In Dahomey,* printed in 1903 by Keith, Prowse, and Co. Ltd., London, England. The chief composer was Will Marion Cook.

pages 18, 43 "The Boll Weevil (De Ballit of De Boll Weevil)" New words and New Music Arrangement by Huddie Ledbetter, collected & adapted by John A. Lomax and Alan Lomax, TRO copyright © 1936 (Renewed) Folkways Music Publishers, Inc., New York, NY. Used by permission.

pages 20, 42 "Lift Ev'ry Voice and Sing,"— James Weldon Johnson, J. Rosamond Johnson. Used by permission of Edward B. Marks Music Company.

pages 25, 43 "Take My Hand, Precious Lord," Words and Music by Thomas A. Dorsey, copyright © 1938, Renewed and Assigned to Unichappell Music, Inc. All rights reserved. Reprinted by permission of Warner Bros. Publications, Inc., Miami, FL 33014.

pages 26, 44 "Take the "A" Train," words and music by Billy Strayhorn, copyright © 1941 (Renewed) by Tempo Music, Inc. and Music Sales Corporation (ASCAP) International copyright secured. All rights reserved. Reprinted by permission.

pages 30, 44 "Dog, Dog" by James Bevel and Bernard LaFayette, copyright © 1961, 1963 (Renewed) by Stormking Music Inc. All rights reserved. Used by permission.

pages 34, 45 "Say It Loud, I'm Black and I'm Proud," Words and Music by James Brown, copyright © 1968, Dynatone Music Publishing Co. (BMI). All rights administered by Unichappell Music, Inc. All rights reserved. Reprinted by permission of Warner Bros. Publications, Inc., Miami, FL 33014.

pages 36, 45 "Happy Birthday," Words and Music by Stevie Wonder, copyright © 1980 Jobete Music Co., Inc., and Black Bull Music Inc. All rights reserved. Reprinted by permission of Warner Bros. Publications, Inc., Miami, FL 33014.